MODERN ROLE MODELS

Jeff Gordon

Kerrily Sapet

Mason Crest Publishers

Produced by OTTN Publishing in association with
21st Century Publishing and Communications, Inc.

MASON CREST PUBLISHERS INC.
370 Reed Road
Broomall, Pennsylvania 19008
(866) MCP-BOOK (toll free)
www.masoncrest.com

Printed in the United States of America.

First Printing

9 8 7 6 5 4 3 2 1

Library of Congress Cataloging-in-Publication Data

Sapet, Kerrily, 1972–
    Jeff Gordon / Kerrily Sapet.
        p. cm. — (Modern role models)
    Includes index.
    ISBN 978-1-4222-0489-4 (hardcover) — ISBN 978-1-4222-0769-7 (pbk.)
    1. Gordon, Jeff, 1971–   —Juvenile literature. 2. Automobile racing drivers—
United States—Biography—Juvenile literature. I. Title.
GV1032.G67S27 2009
796.72092—dc22
[B]   2008025061

Publisher's note:
All quotations in this book come from original sources, and contain the spelling
and grammatical inconsistencies of the original text.

CROSS-CURRENTS

*In the ebb and flow of the currents of life we are each influenced
by many people, places, and events that we directly experience
or have learned about. Throughout the chapters of this book you
will come across CROSS-CURRENTS reference boxes. These
boxes direct you to a CROSS-CURRENTS section in the back
of the book that contains fascinating and informative sidebars
and related pictures. Go on.* ▶▶

CONTENTS

Jeff Gordon celebrates winning NASCAR's Winston Cup Championship in 2001. The Winston Cup series—now known as the Sprint Cup series—is the most important title for stock car drivers. NASCAR drivers earn points for their finishes in races throughout the year; at the end of each season, the driver with the most points wins the championship.

A Four-Time Champion

JEFF GORDON HAS ESTABLISHED HIMSELF AS ONE of the greatest race car drivers in history. The winner of four Winston Cup championship titles, Jeff has frequently topped the list as the number one National Association for **Stock Car** Auto Racing (NASCAR) driver. With 81 career victories, Jeff holds numerous records and awards.

Jeff has won more money than any other NASCAR driver, earning millions for his skill behind the wheel, and more by advertising for numerous companies. Off the track, Jeff donates time and money to charity. Despite his success, Jeff continues his quest to remain one of the best drivers ever.

⋙ THE DRIVING ACE ⋘

One way to measure a NASCAR driver's ability is by the number of championship titles he wins. A driver's reputation also is based on the races he wins. Drivers compete in 36 events throughout the season, but people consider some races more prestigious than others. A few of the most famous are the Daytona 500 in February, the Coca-Cola 600 in May, and the Brickyard 400 in August. Certain races are popular with fans and drivers because of the size and age of the track, the length of the race, the prize money available, and when the race occurs. By 1999, Jeff had captured victories at many of NASCAR's biggest races. He'd won the Southern 500 four times, the Coca-Cola 600 three times, and the Daytona 500 and the Brickyard 400 two times each.

CROSS-CURRENTS

To learn more about the history of stock car racing in the United States, read "NASCAR Nuts and Bolts." Go to page 48. ▶▶

Jeff first climbed into the cockpit of a race car at four years old. After 18 years of breaking records on the racetrack, he burst onto the NASCAR scene in 1993. During an amazing winning **streak** from 1995 to 1998, Jeff dominated the track, winning 40 races and three Winston Cup titles. He seemed to be invincible. With many years of racing ahead of him, people wondered how much more he would achieve. However, Jeff experienced a major change in his career in 1999. That was the year when Jeff's longtime crew chief, Ray Evernham, left the team to become a race car owner.

≫ FACING CHALLENGES ≪

For years, Ray had planned strategies during Jeff's races and managed Jeff's speedy **pit crew**—they could change four tires and fuel a car in under 15 seconds. With Ray gone, many members of Jeff's crew left to work for a competing driver who offered more money. Making matters worse, doctors diagnosed Rick Hendrick, the owner of Jeff's car, with **leukemia**, a type of cancer.

Jeff and his new crew chief, Robbie Loomis, faced more than just building a new pit crew. The Goodyear tire company had developed new racing tires, and Chevrolet had redesigned the type of stock car Jeff drove. In the first race of the 2000 season, Jeff smashed his car during practice. More accidents, wrecks, and pit crew mistakes followed.

In each race during the season, drivers can earn anywhere from 185 points for finishing first to 34 points for finishing last. Officials award extra points to drivers who lead **laps** during the race. The driver with the most points at the end of the season wins the championship title. Jeff only won three races in 2000. He finished ninth in the points

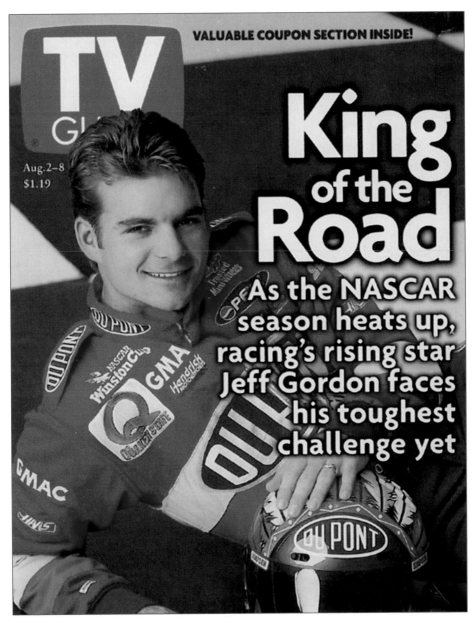

VALUABLE COUPON SECTION INSIDE!

TV GUIDE

Aug. 2–8
$1.19

King of the Road

As the NASCAR season heats up, racing's rising star Jeff Gordon faces his toughest challenge yet

Jeff Gordon became a household name during the mid-1990s, thanks to his regular wins in NASCAR races. Here, he is featured on a 1997 issue of *TV Guide*. Between 1995 and 1998, Jeff dominated NASCAR racing's Winston Cup circuit. He won the championship in 1995, 1997, and 1998, and finished second in 1996.

standings, his worst rank in seven years. For many drivers, finishing ninth would be a satisfactory achievement. Ninth was so far below what people expected of Jeff, however, that many believed his career was over. Jeff and his team were determined to improve, however. Jeff told reporters:

> **❝We've been put to the test before. This is just another test, another challenge. We've never backed away from a challenge. We're not here to prove anything to anybody . . . Our goal is to win races, and win championships. ❞**

⋙ VICTORY LANE ⋘

Jeff's comeback in 2001 began with a defeat. In March, at Georgia's Atlanta Motor Speedway, he lost a race by less than 1/10 of a second. It was the closest finish in NASCAR history. The loss was painful, but the closeness of it was also encouraging, and it sparked a remarkable winning streak. In June, Jeff won races in Delaware and Michigan. By July, he tied driver Dale Jarrett for the points lead. Within a month, Jeff crushed the field of other drivers, winning the Brickyard 400 in Indiana and races in New York and Kansas. Soon he held a massive 349-point lead.

On November 18, at the NAPA 500 at Atlanta Motor Speedway, Jeff clinched his fourth Winston Cup championship title. At 30 years old, he became the youngest four-time champion. He joined Dale Earnhardt Sr. and Richard Petty as the only men in history to win more than three Winston Cup titles. Jeff proved to doubting fans, his crew, and himself that he could return to the top of the racing world. Jeff said:

CROSS-CURRENTS

Read "Track Talk" if you'd like to find out more about the similarities and differences between American racetracks. Go to page 49. ▶▶

> **❝This championship is a lot different than the first three. The year is so special because of the last two years. We had to rebuild and we had to come together, basically, as a new team. We had to climb the mountain again. Because of all the adversity we have had to overcome . . . it has made this year even sweeter. ❞**

NASCAR drivers race over the Atlanta Motor Speeday during the NAPA 500, November 18, 2001. Although Jeff's DuPont-sponsored Chevrolet (marked with the white arrow) is back in the pack in this photo, the young driver finished the race in sixth place. That finish was good enough to secure Jeff's fourth Winston Cup title.

In 2001, Jeff won a record $10 million, topping the all-time prize money list. He also became the first three-time winner of the Brickyard 400. He captured a record seven wins on road courses and completed the season with the most wins, top-five, and top-ten finishes of any driver. Despite the challenges, it had been a record-setting season.

Jeff Gordon was about 18 when he posed for this photo after winning a sprint car race at Indianapolis Raceway Park. From a young age, Jeff proved to be a talented driver. He often won quarter-midget and go-kart races against older kids before moving up to sprint cars. The skills he learned helped him become a successful stock car racer.

2

Racing to the Top

JEFFREY MICHAEL GORDON WAS BORN ON
August 4, 1971, in Vallejo, California, near the San
Francisco Bay. His parents, Carol and Bill Gordon,
also had a four-year-old daughter, Kim. However,
Jeff's parents soon divorced. After this, Carol married
John Bickford, who designed vehicles for people
with disabilities. John also loved car racing.

By the time Jeff was four, he had a BMX racing bike. He played
on jumps at a nearby dirt track and began to compete in races. After
seeing children injured during races, Carol decided BMX was too
dangerous. However, she couldn't stop Jeff's need for speed.

⇛ BORN TO RACE ⇚

Soon John brought home two quarter-midget cars, six-foot-long
cars with open wheels and roll cages. It wasn't long before Jeff was
zooming around a homemade track built from hay bales. At age five,

he flipped his car at a turn during a race. After repairs, he crashed two more times in the same spot. He kept trying until he learned how to make the turn.

Jeff's mother and stepfather encouraged him. John often drove him 50 miles to the track to practice. Jeff loved to race against John's stopwatch, trying to beat his own times. Carol also helped him develop his skills. Driving the other quarter-midget car, she tailed him, cut him off, and weaved in front of him.

≫ DEFEATING THE COMPETITION ≪

Within a year Jeff won 35 events and a championship. His family traveled to races nearly every weekend, often sleeping in their truck. Jeff won so often that other parents accused him of cheating and being too small to race. Jeff said:

> **"When I was four, I looked like a two year old . . . When I realized I was just as good as the older kids, I wanted to spend every spare minute racing. Winning was fun, even for a kid who could barely read the words on the trophies he was getting."**

By 1979 Jeff had set eight records and captured another championship. He began racing go-karts, which required more skill. He won four national titles, defeating 17-year-olds, who started refusing to race him.

Jeff claimed every possible quarter-midget and go-kart award. Then he read about a 13-year-old who raced lightweight sprint cars with 800-**horsepower** engines, about four times more powerful than the average car. Although Jeff couldn't race sprint cars in California until he was 16, racetracks in the Midwest had fewer age restrictions. His parents built him a sprint car with a special seat so Jeff could reach the pedals and steer.

≫ MOVING ON ≪

When Jeff was 14, he and his family moved to Pittsboro, Indiana, a small farm town near Indianapolis Motor Speedway. They lived on their dwindling savings and Jeff's winnings. Having learned mechanical skills from John, Jeff made and sold car parts to keep his sprint car running. He became the youngest driver awarded a

Young drivers are lined up for the start of a go-kart competition. Jeff was eight years old when he started racing go-karts, and he soon won several national titles in the sport. Like Jeff, many other NASCAR drivers got their start racing go-karts, including Darrell Waltrip, Ricky Rudd, and Tony Stewart.

license by the United States Auto Club (USAC), the organization that oversees sprint car racing.

During Jeff's years at Tri-West High, he traveled as far as Florida and Oregon for races on weekends. His parents wanted him to go to college, but Jeff wanted to become a full-time driver. In 1989, on the day of his graduation, Jeff had an important race against the top drivers in the region. He and his parents decided if he raced well, he could compete full-time. If not, he would go to college. Jeff succeeded, and his racing career began.

⟫ CHOOSING HIS RACING FUTURE ⟪

Jeff began to race full-sized midget cars and soon became the youngest driver to win the USAC Midget Championship. In 1990, at a driving school founded by stock car racing champion Buck Baker, Jeff drove a stock car for the first time. Jeff said:

> **❝I loved stock car racing. It was the first time I'd raced anything that big, heavy, and full-bodied. . . . This was old-fashioned racing with big machines that had big rumbling engines and lots of metal.❞**

Jeff's skill impressed car owner Bill Davis, who offered him a contract to race stock cars in NASCAR's Busch series. The Busch, later renamed the Nationwide, is considered NASCAR's minor league for new drivers. Premier drivers compete in NASCAR's Winston Cup series. In 1991, Jeff began working with crew chief Ray Evernham and became the Busch series **Rookie** of the Year. Soon he signed a contract with Rick Hendrick, owner of Hendrick Motorsports racing team, to drive in the Winston Cup series. Emblazoned with a number 24, Jeff's powerful car featured bright rainbow colors.

CROSS-CURRENTS

For a better understanding of the differences between regular cars and stock cars, read "Under the Hood." Go to page 50. ▶▶

⟫ A CAREER BEGINS ⟪

In the final race of 1992, Jeff's Winston Cup career began—and Richard Petty's ended. Reporters compared the rookie and the legend. Jeff said:

> **❝I'd like to think that someday when people think of me, they would say just one-hundredth of the nice things they say about Richard. . . . I think it's really neat to have your name mentioned with him, but . . . I'm just trying to be Jeff Gordon.❞**

At the start of 1993, Jeff won the Gatorade 125, making him the youngest driver ever to qualify for the Daytona 500. Drivers teased him when he didn't know how to get to **Victory Lane** to celebrate his win. Jeff captured the attention of the media and Brooke Sealey,

Legendary stock car driver Richard Petty stands next to a life-sized wax figure of himself at Las Vegas Motor Speedway. During his long NASCAR career, Petty won 200 races, more than any other driver in history. He also won seven championships. The final race of Petty's career in 1992 was also Jeff Gordon's first Winston Cup race.

the model who presented his trophy. The two began dating.

At the Daytona 500 Jeff led the first lap, which no rookie had ever done. He finished fifth, setting the NASCAR world abuzz. At the season's end, he ranked 14th and became Rookie of the Year. Jeff had found success.

CROSS-CURRENTS

Check out "Drive-through Service" to learn more about the important job of a driver's pit crew. Go to page 51. ▶▶

Jeff often credits his racing success to his pit crew. "I've had to learn a lot of things very quickly, and I try to learn from [my] mistakes," he said after winning the Winston Cup title in 1995. "You've got to fight hard to win a championship, and we all did it as a team together."

3

Dominating the Track

JEFF GORDON STARTED THE 1994 SEASON HUNGRY for his first Winston Cup series win. He had spent the off-season practicing. He trained on the track, driving laps and testing cars, while his pit crew made mechanical adjustments. Jeff also worked out in the gym to become physically and mentally stronger.

Determined, he and his crew worked hard to succeed. Ray Evernham, Jeff's crew chief, hung up motivating signs to encourage the team. Jeff's favorite was a simple to-do list—climb up from a nobody to a winner to a champion to a racing legend.

⇒ WONDER BOY ⇐

Despite their hopes, the 1994 season began with a string of rocky races. Jeff finished fourth in the Daytona 500. Then, during a Virginia race, Jeff's crew didn't tighten the lug nuts on his left front tire. Although the tire rolled off as he pulled away, he finished third. He finished eighth at a race at Atlanta Motor Speedway, but then a wreck at

CROSS-CURRENTS

To get a view of a race from Jeff Gordon's perspective, check out "In the Driver's Seat." Go to page 52. ▶▶

Talladega **Superspeedway** caused him to finish 40th. The team couldn't clinch a win.

Jeff's team finally got their victory in May at Lowe's Motor Speedway in North Carolina. During Jeff's final pit stop, Ray changed only two of Jeff's tires, getting him back out on the track in 9.5 seconds. Every second in pit road costs a driver 100 feet on the track. Ray's decision gave Jeff the edge he needed to win the Coca-Cola 600. With tears in his eyes, Jeff pulled into Victory Lane for the first time in a Winston Cup race.

In August, Jeff competed in the Brickyard 400, the first NASCAR race held at Indianapolis Motor Speedway. (The track is nicknamed the Brickyard because it was originally paved with bricks in 1909.) Growing up near the speedway, Jeff remembered watching his favorite drivers from behind the fence surrounding Gasoline Alley, where the teams' garages were located. Now he was a driver here. In a race before nearly 350,000 spectators, Jeff captured his second victory. Choked with emotion, he took an extra victory lap so no one would see him crying. He said:

> **"**I'll tell you, this is a great day. I hope that I'm here at the Indianapolis Speedway all day long. I'm in a candy store, I've got a big smile on my face. . . . I don't know what to say. It's just far past any words that can describe the way I feel.**"**

Competing against more experienced drivers, Jeff had won two of the most prestigious Winston Cup races. He finished eighth in the points standings. On November 25, at the end of the season, he and Brooke married in Charlotte, North Carolina. Other drivers nicknamed him Wonder Boy, because of his youth and success. The name would stick with Jeff for years.

➤ A YOUNG CHAMPION ◀

Jeff's 1995 season started strong. By May, he had won four races and was ranked number one in the standings for the first time. Dale Earnhardt Sr. trailed him closely, and the media rumbled about a rivalry.

Brooke Sealey gives Jeff a hug and kiss after the young driver won the first Brickyard 400 at Indianapolis Motor Speedway, August 6, 1994. Brooke and Jeff met in 1993 after he won a qualifying race for the Daytona 500. They soon began dating, and married in November 1994.

Earnhardt was an aggressive driver with a tough, gritty image. By contrast, Jeff seemed polite and clean-cut. He attracted a new generation of fans. To many, however, Jeff was an outsider. He came from California, not typically home to NASCAR drivers. They said his success came too easily. Unlike other drivers, he had advantages: family support, Ray Evernham's mechanical ability, Rick Hendrick's wealth, and a well-trained pit crew, the Rainbow Warriors, in their colorful uniforms. Jeff's stepfather disagreed with accusations that Jeff hadn't earned his fame:

> **"We slept in pick-up trucks and made our own parts. . . . Jeff is misunderstood by people who think he was born to rich parents and had a silver spoon in his mouth. The laps he drove when he was 6 or 7 years old, he's still applying them."**

Some fans yelled insults, hurled things at Jeff's car, and cheered when he crashed. Earnhardt told him that as long as people were making noise—either cheering or booing—it meant he was winning. For years Jeff would be both the favorite and the least favorite driver in NASCAR. Some drivers criticized the abusive fans. Mark Martin said:

> **"I am, in a lot of ways, a Jeff Gordon fan. I approve of him, the way he lives his life, the way he conducts himself, and everything else. . . . It hurts me to hear him booed because he's good."**

In 1995, Jeff won nine **pole position** starts. The fastest driver in **qualifying races** wins the best starting position for the main race—the pole position on the first row on the inside of the track. This good position helped Jeff win seven races, more than any other driver. On November 12, at Atlanta Motor Speedway, Jeff captured his first Winston Cup championship title, edging out Earnhardt by just 34 points. At 24, Jeff was the youngest driver ever to win the championship.

⟫ FAST FAME ⟪

With Jeff's Winston Cup title came a whirlwind of fame. **Sponsors** clamored for Jeff to advertise their products. The media wanted photo shoots and interviews. Jeff had little privacy and little time to spend with family and friends.

Jeff carefully planned his daily schedule. During the off-season, he gave speeches, afterwards signing up to 600 autographs in three hours. He appeared in advertisements for sponsors such as Pepsi and DuPont. Jeff tested cars for the upcoming season, met with his crew, and spent rare days relaxing at home. During the season, he focused on each upcoming race. Every Thursday for 36 weeks, Jeff arrived at a different racetrack and prepared for the race. For the next three nights, he slept in the rear bedroom of a luxurious motor home.

Jeff learned to live up to the fame and the expectations. His success continued into 1996. He captured eight wins and finished in the top ten in all but eight races. Mechanical problems in the last race of the season ended his chances of overtaking driver Terry Labonte for the championship title. At the end of the season Jeff stood in second place.

Jeff Gordon (number 24) edges past Dale Earnhardt Sr. (number 3) during a NASCAR race at the Atlanta Motor Speedway. For many years Earnhardt had been NASCAR's best driver, until Jeff emerged to challenge his position atop the sport. Although the two drivers liked and respected each other, they competed fiercely on the track.

During the mid-1990s, Jeff became famous for his rainbow-colored race cars. However, his cars sometimes sported different colors and images. For example, he entered this car—painted to promote a theme park ride—in a May 1997 race at Charlotte Motor Speedway. No matter what his car looked like, Jeff often found himself in Victory Lane during 1997.

Jeff's 1997 season, one of the best of his career, began with a victory at the Daytona 500. At 25, he was the youngest driver ever to win the race. By June, he tied Labonte for the points lead. Jeff soon had seven wins. No other driver had more than two. In August, he won the Southern 500 at Darlington Raceway in South Carolina and claimed a $1 million bonus for winning three of NASCAR's most prestigious races that year. On November 16, Jeff clinched his second Winston Cup championship title, becoming the youngest driver to capture two titles. In the past two years, Jeff had won 17 races, more than the next two drivers combined.

⟫ UPS AND DOWNS ⟪

The 1998 season began with a loss to Dale Earnhardt Sr. at the Daytona 500. A small piece of debris had damaged Jeff's car and cost him the race. Although frustrated, Jeff said:

> **"We all would have loved to have been in Victory Lane, but we're all real happy for Dale. If we couldn't be there, we all loved for him to be. He earned it. . . . He deserves it."**

Jeff and his team quickly rebounded and began winning. By May he led in the points race. In September, he won the Southern 500 and claimed the $1 million bonus. He drove around the track behind a truck spewing fake million dollar bills that pictured him. On November 8, Jeff won his third championship title with a 364-point lead. He became the youngest three-time champion. In just four years, Jeff had tied Richard Petty's record of winning 13 races in one season. Jeff had won 40 races and finished in the top ten 98 times.

Jeff's 1999 season began well. With 12 laps to go in the Daytona 500, less than half a second separated the top cars. A risky pass on the apron, the paved area between the track and the **infield**, gave Jeff the edge he needed to win. For the rest of the season, though, Jeff faced car troubles and accidents. At Texas Motor Speedway his car slammed into a wall, badly bruising his ribs. Then, Jeff's crew chief, Ray, decided to start his own racing team. At the same time, the Rainbow Warriors left to work for competitor Dale Jarrett.

CROSS-CURRENTS
For more information about some of the greatest stock car drivers of all time, read "Legendary Racers." Go to page 53. ▶▶

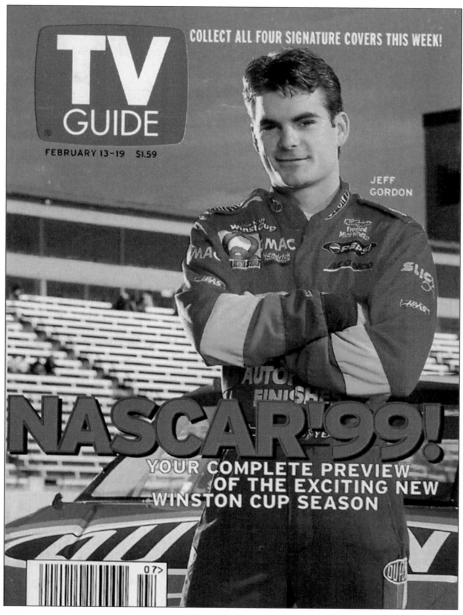

TV Guide featured Jeff on the cover of its 1999 NASCAR season preview issue. However, after winning back-to-back Winston Cup championships, 1999 proved to be a disappointing season for Jeff. Although he did win seven races and finish in the top five 18 times, he slipped to sixth in the season rankings.

⟫ OVERCOMING THE CHALLENGES ⟪

Jeff and his new crew chief, Robbie Loomis, worked to build a new crew. They also adjusted to the new tires Goodyear developed and the new design of Chevrolets. Jeff helped motivate and lead his rookie crew, as they learned to work quickly together in the pits. It took nearly a year for the team to begin winning again. At the end of 2000, he ranked ninth in the standings, his worst finish since his rookie year.

The next year started with Jeff getting tangled up in a wreck in the Daytona 500. Later, in the same race, he watched as Dale Earnhardt Sr. crashed into a wall. The impact and angle of the collision fatally injured Earnhardt. Although Jeff and Earnhardt were fierce competitors, Jeff was saddened by his friend's death. Fans wouldn't forget Earnhardt and his legendary number 3 car.

Despite the dismal start, Jeff's team began winning. They quickly moved into the points lead. More success followed, including a victory at the Brickyard 400. At the end of the 2001 season, Jeff claimed his fourth championship title. Not only had he won a record amount of money, but people began comparing him to racing legends Richard Petty and Dale Earnhardt Sr., who had both won seven titles. Although a champion, Jeff remained humble and grateful for his team. His crew chief Robbie said:

> **Jeff Gordon makes you want to do a better job. His ability and his compassionate heart, the way he treats people . . . it makes you want to do the very best job possible for that boy. At the end of the day, anything short of winning, you haven't done your job because he's capable of winning every race he starts.**

During the year, Jeff also turned to helping others. He had watched Ray Evernham's son and Rick Hendrick battle leukemia. In 1999 he established the Jeff Gordon Foundation, an organization that raises money and helps fund programs for children with life-threatening diseases. Watching others face serious illnesses helped Jeff put his troubles on the track into perspective.

Jeff suffered through difficult years in 2002 and 2003. "You go through times when you work just as hard and are doing everything the same, and [winning is] just not happening," he admitted in 2002. "You just start to question a lot of things, but my confidence in my driving, I don't think that I ever really questioned that."

Tough Times

FOR 26 YEARS JEFF HAD DEDICATED HIS LIFE TO racing, thriving on competition. He loved to cross the finish line first and see the black-and-white **checkered flag** officials waved for the winning driver. With four Winston Cup championship titles (the fourth coming in 2001), Jeff had achieved more fame and fortune than most drivers in the history of racing.

Jeff's rise to fame hadn't always been easy. During the previous two years, his abilities to drive and to lead a team had been tested. Jeff and his crew had risen to the challenge. The strong new team had helped Jeff win his fourth championship. In the years ahead though, Jeff would face difficult times on and off the track.

⇒ RUMORS ⇐

Jeff and his wife Brooke had been married for eight years, but in 2002 the couple separated and planned to divorce. News of Jeff's impending divorce spread rapidly. Soon rumors and gossip about Jeff and Brooke splashed across the headlines of newspapers and magazines. During interviews, reporters asked Jeff questions about his private life and his divorce, instead of his driving.

Jeff and Brooke had purchased a mansion in Florida and employed a chef, a maid, and a gardener. They also owned several expensive cars and a boat. During court proceedings that grew increasingly difficult and embarrassing, Jeff moved out of the house and Brooke received much of the property. Reporters exposed many of the details of the divorce to the public.

Jeff moved in with a friend in Charlotte, North Carolina, near Jeff's offices at Hendrick Motorsports. The world-famous driver slept on his friend's couch during the week and traveled to racetracks on the weekends. He relied on his friends and family for support. Despite his difficult divorce, he still faced his own high expectations on the track, along with those of his crew and his fans.

➤ TROUBLE ON THE TRACK ◀

In the midst of Jeff's personal troubles, he also struggled behind the wheel. He went the first half of the 2002 season without a victory, not winning a race in 24 starts. It was Jeff's longest losing streak since his Winston Cup career began. The media focused on Jeff's stretch of bad luck. They linked his troubles on the track to his divorce, although Jeff told reporters that he only focused on driving once he climbed into his race car. Jeff's stepfather John offered an explanation, though:

> **❝If you get up in the morning and you're already not happy, you're not going to do your best work. But if life is perfect and everything is going your way, then you're going to do your job well, which for Jeff is to drive a car and communicate with his team.❞**

Trouble followed Jeff and his pit crew during races that year. In April, at Martinsville Speedway in Virginia, a flat tire and problems with his car's steering caused him to finish in 23rd place. Two months later, after having difficulties with his car's gears, he limped across the finish line in 37th place. More mechanical snags followed.

Many factors—from the inside to the outside of the car—affect its speed. The car's frame, engine, gears, tires, and much more play a part. When all of the parts are working well together, the car can reach its top speed. When they're not, the car is harder to control and goes slower. But Jeff remained positive and told reporters:

"There's no doubt [going through a difficult divorce] affects you," Jeff told *Sports Illustrated* during the 2002 season. **"How could it not? But I've had a lot of things that have been distractions throughout the years, and I've won races and won championships."** Nevertheless, the 2002 season was frustrating for Jeff, as he only won three races.

JEFF GORDON

> **"If my experience has shown me anything, it's that good people can rise to meet any challenge. Our team proved that . . . and we're proving it again every weekend we compete. . . . I believe that life is a very long race, one with a lot of good runs, and a few bad ones. The team and I are ready for the next challenge."**

With three wins and a few close finishes, Jeff ended the 2002 season in fourth place. During the year, people compared Jeff to the rising star Jimmie Johnson, who also raced for the Hendrick Motorsports team. Jimmie had quickly racked up three victories and

Jeff talks with rookie driver Jimmie Johnson (right) in the garage at the Daytona International Speedway, 2002. Jeff was co-owner of Jimmie's car, and served as a mentor for the younger driver. Off the track, the two men became good friends.

four pole positions, along with becoming the first rookie ever to lead in the point standings. In the past few years, Jeff had become both a driver and a car owner. He and Rick Hendrick owned the car that Johnson drove as he swiftly defeated competitors.

Despite any rivalries on the track, Jeff and Jimmie became friends. They relied on each other for advice. As teammates, they could also help each other during races by drafting, which is when one car follows directly behind another. The car in front cuts through the air, helping to pull the second car forward, making it go even faster. Sometimes cars draft so closely they actually touch. Although both drivers are out to win, at times during races they have the opportunity to help their teammates.

CROSS-CURRENTS

To find out how Jeff and other NASCAR drivers prepare for a competition, read "Training to Race." Go to page 53. ▶▶

⟫ DIFFICULT SEASONS ⟪

Although talk buzzed about Jimmie Johnson and Dale Earnhardt Jr., the son of Dale Earnhardt Sr., Jeff remained wildly popular. In 2003 he wrote two books—*Jeff Gordon: Burning Up the Track* and *Jeff Gordon: Racing Back to the Front*. Both books traced his life as a driver. He also appeared on late-night television shows and sometimes hosted a morning television show. He opened a car dealership in North Carolina and released the Jeff Gordon Monte Carlo car. Fans snapped up the midnight-blue cars and had Jeff sign the car's dashboard.

Although people talked about Jeff struggling, in August of 2003 he won the Brickyard 400 at Indianapolis Motor Speedway. It was his fourth win at the event. Jeff joined only three other men in history to win four times at the speedway—Indy car racing legends A.J. Foyt, Rick Mears, and Al Unser. At the end of the year Jeff finished the season with three wins, and again ranked fourth.

The next year Jeff remained even closer in the point standings. But on October 24, 2004, tragedy struck his team. On the way to a race, a private Hendrick Motorsports plane crashed in thick fog. Several of Rick Hendrick's family members were killed in the crash: his brother, his two nieces, and his son Ricky. Other key employees also lost their lives. It was of course a huge personal tragedy to Rick. It was also a tremendous loss to Jeff and the Hendrick Motorsports team. Fans left flowers and messages at the gates surrounding the company's offices.

Jeff often acted as a spokesman for the company, speaking eloquently about the family's loss and thanking their supporters. He focused on the importance of continuing with their jobs on the track, however, as that was important to all of the Hendricks. Although it was tough to carry on, the team forged ahead. Jeff did his part, winning a total of five races and finishing third at the end of the season.

HITTING BOTTOM

On the heels of their personal tragedy, Jeff and his team found success when he captured a victory at the Daytona 500 in 2005. During the 500-mile race, Jeff managed to edge out leading driver Dale Earnhardt Jr. In the final nine laps of the race, the lead changed four times, but Jeff held off Earnhardt and driver Kurt Busch for the win. The team seemed to be back on track.

More wins quickly followed. In April 2005, Jeff won a race at Martinsville Speedway. Next he won the Aaron's 499 at Talladega Superspeedway. Jeff and his team seemed to have shaken off their long streak of bad luck. Fans and reporters began talking about a Drive for Five, as Jeff sped toward his fifth Winston Cup championship title.

By late spring, however, the talk and the momentum came to a halt when Jeff's slump returned. He and his crew struggled with ongoing car problems. From the middle of May to the middle of July he finished 30th or worse in six races. He had a stretch of 21 races without even a top-five finish. Jeff said:

> **"I'm looking at this [2005] season this way: The first half really hasn't gone that well, but I'm not that far out of the lead. Imagine what will happen if we get some things going our way. I know how this team is. If we get a win, watch out. "**

STARTING OVER

In September Jeff's team changed crew chiefs. Many teams announce changes at the end of the season. Jeff's crew chief Robbie Loomis took a job working for Petty Enterprises, run by racing king Richard Petty. Robbie wanted a less stressful job working as a team advisor. Before leaving, he trained Steve Letarte as Jeff's new crew chief. Steve took over for the last ten races of the 2005 season.

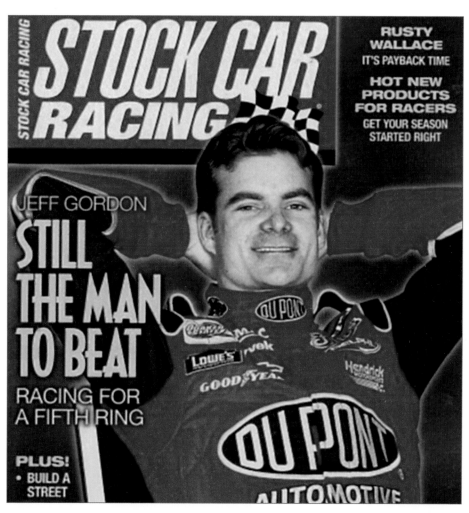

STOCK CAR RACING

STOCK CAR RACING

RUSTY WALLACE
IT'S PAYBACK TIME

HOT NEW PRODUCTS FOR RACERS
GET YOUR SEASON STARTED RIGHT

JEFF GORDON

STILL THE MAN TO BEAT

RACING FOR A FIFTH RING

PLUS!
• BUILD A STREET

DU PONT AUTOMOTIVE

Despite his struggles, Jeff usually found himself in the hunt for the NASCAR title. A fifth win in the championship series—renamed the Nextel Cup before the 2004 season—eluded Jeff, however. He finished fourth in 2002 and 2003, and third in 2004. In 2005, Jeff had one of his worst seasons, finishing 11th in the Nextel Cup standings.

The team made changes to improve the way Jeff's car handled. Just five races later, at Martinsville Speedway, they captured their first win since April. Two top-five finishes followed in the last four races of the season.

CROSS-CURRENTS

Read "Sports Speak" if you would like a quick lesson in the terminology of auto racing. Go to page 54. ▶▶

JEFF GORDON

By the end of the dismal season, Jeff had won a total of four races and finished 11th in the standings. In the last ten races of the year, nicknamed the Chase for the Championship, only the top ten drivers were eligible to win the title. But Jeff's worst season since 1993 ended

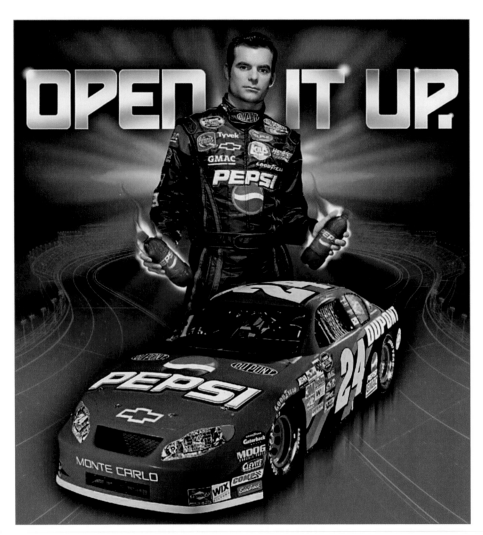

Because of his position as one of stock car racing's best drivers, as well as his clean-cut image, many companies want Jeff to promote their products. Since 1997, Pepsi has been one of Jeff's biggest sponsors. He appears in their national advertisements, and drives a Pepsi-themed car in two NASCAR races each season.

on an encouraging note with a win and two strong finishes. The team was driven to improve the next year and had high hopes for the upcoming Daytona 500.

There was another highlight to Jeff's frustrating season. Jeff had met Ingrid Vandebosch, a model from Belgium, at a friend's vacation home. She had moved to the United States in 1992 and knew little about car racing. The two started dating in 2004 and continued seeing each other during 2005.

Throughout the tough year, Jeff continued his charity work. Many groups noted Jeff's involvement and interest in aiding others. *USA Today* newspaper named him the Most Caring Athlete and he was named NASCAR's Good Guy of the Year. Jeff also received further recognition and awards from many charities. Working with others helped put Jeff's own troubles in perspective. He said:

> **"One thing I'd learned from my past struggles was that you never know when your next win is going to come, so you need to appreciate the moment. I'd also been reminded that we aren't promised tomorrow."**

Jeff stands next to his car before a 2006 race at Texas Motor Speedway. After a terrible season in 2005, Jeff hoped that working with a new crew chief would help turn things around. Although he only won two races in 2006, Jeff finished in the top five 14 times. He placed sixth in the Nextel Cup standings.

5

The Drive for Five

THE YEARS BETWEEN 2002 AND 2005 WERE difficult for Jeff. He suffered through a much-publicized divorce from his wife of eight years. He and his teammates at Hendrick Motorsports lost family and friends in a plane crash. Accidents and mechanical failures during races often kept Jeff out of Victory Lane.

Many people connected the trouble in Jeff's personal life to his problems behind the wheel. Others cited ongoing problems with his car and its handling. Either way, Jeff and his new crew chief, Steve Letarte, were determined to start fresh in the 2006 season.

⇛ BIG CHANGES ⇚

Jeff and Steve had first met when Steve was 16 years old and sweeping floors in the Hendrick Motorsports garage. Since then, Steve had worked his way up through the ranks. A gutsy, smart mechanic,

Steve had bold plans to improve Jeff's car. He ripped up two years' worth of notes and began building a new car. He relied on the Hendrick Motorsports engine department and on the chassis department, which builds the framework of each car. Even small changes would make a big difference in how Jeff's race car performed. After each race, mechanics took the engine apart. They tested it and replaced certain parts, like the pistons and valves, every time. They reused or rebuilt other parts. The typical race car engine only runs 15 to 20 times before it is retired. Jeff and Steve soon communicated well with each other, which is important for a successful team. As Jeff put it:

> **Steve could dissect what I was saying and get a mental picture of what was happening in the car. I won a lot of races with Ray Evernham, but I've never been around anyone who can get on the same page with me as fast as Steve.**

As mechanics made key adjustments to Jeff's car, other important changes occurred for Jeff. After dating for more than a year, he and Ingrid announced that they planned to marry. Jeff had found happiness in his personal life off the track.

Throughout 2006 Jeff's season continued to improve. In the spring, he finished second in races at Martinsville Speedway and Darlington Raceway. In June, Jeff captured a win at Infineon Raceway in California. In July, he had his first win at Chicagoland Speedway in Illinois. Jeff ended the year ranked sixth in the standings, a big jump from his 11th place finish in 2005. Jeff and the Hendrick Motorsports team seemed to be back on track.

After a successful year, Jeff and Ingrid married in a small ceremony in Mexico on November 7. Soon, in addition to their home in Charlotte, North Carolina, they bought an apartment in New York City. Both of them enjoyed visiting and touring the city.

➤ A HELPING HAND ◄

Along with Jeff's fame and winnings came the opportunity to make a difference in the world by helping others. Despite his busy life, he often fulfilled the wishes of seriously ill children who hoped to meet him. Through the Make-A-Wish Foundation Jeff invited children

The pit crew jumps into action around Jeff's car during a 2006 race at Bristol Motor Speedway in Tennessee. Jeff hired 26-year-old Steve Letarte as his crew chief in late 2005. Letarte was one of the youngest crew chiefs on the Nextel Cup circuit, but he quickly learned how to help Jeff win.

to attend races. He visited with them, included them in activities before the race, and presented them with special souvenirs. He said:

> **"It's humbling to know that these kids choose to spend time with me. They face tremendous challenges every day because of their conditions, and the strength and determination they show is really inspiring to me. It's just heartwarming to see their smiles and know they are enjoying themselves at a difficult time in their lives."**

JEFF GORDON

Jeff is interviewed after a race at Daytona. Over the years, Jeff has been deeply involved in helping children suffering from chronic or life-threatening diseases. His Jeff Gordon Foundation provides support to such groups as the Leukemia and Lymphoma Society, The Make-A-Wish Foundation, Riley Hospital for Children in Indianapolis, and the Jeff Gordon Children's Hospital in North Carolina.

Jeff frequently raised money by auctioning off his racing souvenirs and one time even his expensive car. He joined other famous athletes such as baseball star Cal Ripken, boxing legend Muhammad Ali, and hockey great Mario Lemieux to help found Athletes for Hope. These sports leaders wanted to encourage more athletes to support charities, volunteer their services, and act as role models.

Through his foundation, Jeff also funded the Jeff Gordon Children's Hospital in North Carolina. Dedicated to helping children with life-threatening diseases, the hospital was designed to make families comfortable during their stay. With calming settings, such as gardens and aquariums, the hospital staff hoped to soothe anxious children and their families.

⋙ SUCCESS ⋘

Jeff's 2007 season would become one of his best ever. In March, he and other drivers competed in a new style of car, called the Car of Tomorrow, or COT. NASCAR had changed its overall car design for the **Sprint Cup series**. After a seven-year design process, sparked by Dale Earnhardt Sr.'s fatal crash, NASCAR officials implemented the larger, boxier car. It had improved safety features, but the changes impacted its handling. In the first race featuring the new Car of Tomorrow, Jeff finished third.

In April he won a race at Phoenix International Raceway in Arizona, his first victory at that track. Next, he won the Aaron's 499 at Talladega Superspeedway. He soon captured wins at Darlington Raceway and at Pocono Raceway in Pennsylvania. Two more wins followed in October. By the end of the year he had six wins, 21 top-five finishes, and a record 30 top-ten finishes.

Although Jeff didn't win the championship title, he finished second to his teammate Jimmie Johnson in the standings. This was Jeff's best ranking in six years. In 2007, Jeff set another record. For 14 consecutive seasons he had captured at least one victory, and often more. This was the longest streak among current drivers. Jeff also had put himself sixth on the all-time wins list when he won his 81st race on October 13.

Beyond his accomplishments on the track, Jeff became a father. In May, he and Ingrid had welcomed their new daughter, Ella Sofia. Jeff said:

> **❝I'm in the best place in my life that I've ever been. That definitely plays a role in how you perform as a race car driver. I'm so happy to have Steve as my crew chief,**

CROSS-CURRENTS

To find out about how fans enjoy watching their favorite drivers race each weekend, read "A Spectator Sport." Go to page 54. ▶▶

CROSS-CURRENTS

Read "Women in NASCAR" to find out about some female drivers who have competed in races with male drivers. Go to page 55. ▶▶

and things couldn't be any better with Ingrid. Hope-
fully we can continue to roll. **"**

⟫ IN THE FAST LANE ⟪

Jeff's return to the top of the racing world generated much attention.
Jeff's fans enjoyed their favorite driver's renewed success. They also
got a peek of what a typical day in Jeff's life looked like. During 2007
Jeff worked on a documentary called *24 x 24: Wide Open with Jeff
Gordon*. The movie featured interviews with Jeff, his family, Rick

**Members of his team soaked Jeff in water and Gatorade
after he won the Dodge Avenger 500 at Darlington Raceway
in South Carolina, May 13, 2007. The 2007 season turned out
to be one of Jeff's best. He won six races and set a NASCAR
record with 30 top-ten finishes.**

Hendrick, Ray Evernham, and others. It offered fans a chance to see what Jeff's life was like on and off the track.

For the 2008 season, Jeff would have a new teammate with Hendrick Motorsports: Dale Earnhardt Jr. The son of Jeff's former friend and mentor had been one of NASCAR's top drivers since 2003. Over the years Jeff and Dale Jr. had occasionally had clashes on the track. However, the two drivers also respected each other.

As 2008 began, Jeff started his 15th season in NASCAR. At the end of February, he finished third in a race in California. The next weekend, though, at Las Vegas Motor Speedway in Nevada, his car spun wildly out of control and slammed into a portion of the track wall that wasn't covered with a soft, protective barrier. Although Jeff wasn't injured in the dangerous accident, he and other drivers demanded that protective barriers completely encircle every track. Some teams spoke of boycotting the track in Las Vegas until officials fixed the problem. Driver safety had come a long way since the beginning of car racing, even in the years since Dale Earnhardt Sr.'s fatal crash it could still improve.

This somewhat rocky beginning to the season didn't diminish Jeff's confidence. By the end of March he and his team had racked up a second-place finish at the Goodys Cool Orange 500 at Martinsville Speedway, even though a crash followed the next week at Texas Motor Speedway. Next he pulled off a third place finish at Darlington Raceway in May. His team performed and communicated well. By the end of June 2008 he ranked sixth in the points race toward the championship. His Hendrick Motorsports teammates Dale Earnhardt Jr. and Jimmie Johnson were ranked third and fifth, respectively. Although Jeff still had not won a race at the midpoint of the 2008 season, he was hopeful that a late-season push could propel him to a fifth championship.

⇒ LOOKING AHEAD ⇐

Although in recent years Jeff has endured difficulties, he remains one of the top drivers ever to race around a NASCAR track. From the time he was four years old, before he even climbed into a stock car, Jeff was breaking records. A full-time driver since 1993, Jeff has captured more than 80 wins, 150 top-five finishes, 200 top-ten finishes, and 40 pole positions. He has won the highest achievement for a NASCAR driver—the championship title—four times,

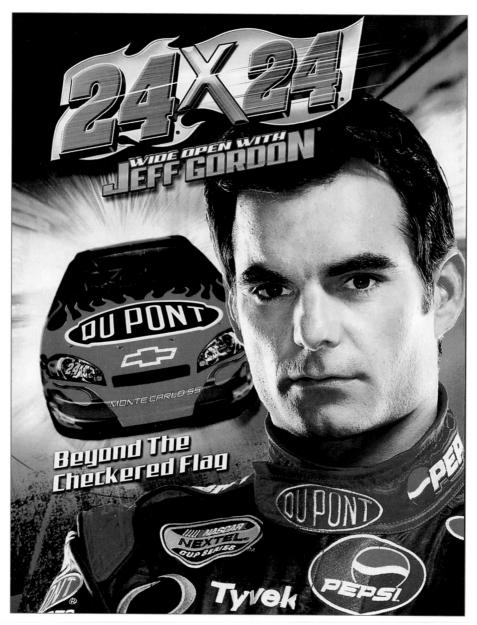

The 2007 documentary *24x24: Wide Open with Jeff Gordon* explores a day in the life of the racing superstar, both on and off the track. The film included an interview with Jeff conducted by actor and race car owner Patrick Dempsey, as well as scenes with family members, other drivers, and friends.

equaling only two other drivers in history. Jeff holds many records in his sport and has won some of NASCAR's most prestigious races, such as the Daytona 500, the Southern 500, and the Brickyard 400 numerous times each. He holds a record nine victories on road courses.

Jeff also considers his charity work to be one of his greatest successes. As the founder of the Jeff Gordon Foundation and co-founder of Athletes for Hope, Jeff has spent much time and money to help children suffering from serious illnesses. He has met with over 200 children from the Make-A-Wish Foundation.

Jeff drives his number 24 car during a 2008 race at Texas Motor Speedway. Since becoming a NASCAR driver in the early 1990s, Jeff Gordon has attracted many new fans to his sport. He has already set many records, and is still young enough to break a number of career marks before he is finished racing.

Jeff holds his one-year-old daughter Ella in the pit area before the start of a June 2008 race. "Being a parent is a lot of hard work and one of the toughest things I've ever done," Jeff admitted that year, "but it's also the most gratifying and exciting thing I've ever been a part of."

In recent years, he has also found happiness in his life with his marriage to Ingrid and the birth of their daughter.

Although he is both loved and despised, most people agree that Jeff Gordon is one of the greatest race car drivers in history. He had achieved immense success at a much younger age than most other drivers. Although few still call him Wonder Boy, Jeff's career could continue for many more years. Many wonder how far he will go toward matching or beating more NASCAR records.

Jeff continues to speed around the track as he has for more than three decades. Ray Evernham once tacked up a quote on the garage wall to motivate Jeff and his team when Jeff first started driving stock cars. The quote tells the story of Jeff's rise to fame behind the wheel:

> **From Nobody to Upstart.**
> **From Upstart to Contender.**
> **From Contender to Winner.**
> **From Winner to Champion.**
> **From Champion to Dynasty.**

NASCAR Nuts and Bolts

With the invention of cars came car racing. As automobiles became more affordable, racing became more popular. Many say that the prohibition of alcohol in the 1920s helped the sport grow, especially in the South. Moonshiners, or people illegally selling alcohol, tried to outrun the police in fast cars. They enjoyed competing against each other, too. Soon fans lined race tracks, sitting in bleachers, cheering their favorite drivers, and munching on hot dogs. Today car racing is popular throughout the world. Millions of people attend races each year, with millions more watching on television.

Over time, different types of race cars developed. Some had open wheels, while others had fenders, like the cars stocked on car lots. In 1948, Bill France founded NASCAR or the National Association for Stock Car Auto Racing.

Today NASCAR sponsors 36 Sprint Cup races each year. Beginning in February, drivers race nearly every Sunday until November. Races range from the 300-mile-long Sylvania 300 to the 600-mile-long Coca-Cola 600. Drivers compete for points, aiming to win the championship. When Jeff won, the championship title was called the Winston Cup. Over the years it's been renamed to the Nextel Cup, and as of 2008, the Sprint Cup. Winning the championship is NASCAR's highest honor.

(Go back to page 6.)

The NASCAR Sprint Cup season includes 36 races held between February and November each year. Drivers earn points based on their finish in each race, as well as the number of laps they lead during the race. After 26 races have been completed, the top 12 drivers compete for the Sprint Cup championship over the last 10 races.

Track Talk

An aerial view of the Bristol Motor Speedway in Tennessee, one of the shortest tracks that host NASCAR Sprint Cup races. It is slightly more than a half-mile around Bristol's oval concrete track. The largest NASCAR racetrack in the United States is Talladega Superspeedway in Alabama. It is 2.66 miles around Talladega's asphalt track.

Early race car drivers raced on surfaces from winding roads, dirt tracks at county fairs, paths plowed in farmer's fields, and stretches of sandy beaches. Wooden tracks eventually gave way to smoothly paved speedways, allowing drivers to reach speeds of more than 200 miles per hour. Today's drivers mostly race on paved, oval-shaped tracks and roads.

NASCAR drivers speed around 22 different tracks. Short tracks, like Bristol Motor Speedway in Tennessee, are less than one mile long. Intermediate tracks, like Darlington Raceway in South Carolina, are between one and two miles long. Superspeedways, like Talladega in Alabama, are greater than two miles in length.

Drivers make only left turns on tracks, but on road courses they turn both left and right.

Tracks feature straightaways and curves that slope steeply at the corners. Pit road, where crews service the cars, is usually along the first straightaway. The area between the track and the infield is called the apron. Each track also has a Victory Lane, a spot on the infield where winners park their car to celebrate. While early tracks had few safety precautions, most today have soft barriers that protect both the drivers and the spectators watching the race either from the infield or the grandstands.

(Go back to page 8.)

Under the Hood

Race cars aren't much like the cars average people buy. But most people don't cover 500 miles in three hours. NASCAR drivers race Dodges, Fords, Chevrolets, and Toyotas—all with modifications to make them speedier and safer.

Race cars have heavy-duty brakes and powerful engines. Special fans cool the brakes to keep them from disintegrating. Lightweight racing tires, able to withstand high heat, have extra grip and traction, making them sticky to the touch. The cars sit lower, which gives them better handling control and makes them more aerodynamic. Race cars also are equipped with roof flaps to keep them from becoming airborne.

Race cars don't have doors. A removable steering wheel makes it easier for drivers to climb in and out of the cockpit. To start their engines, drivers don't turn keys. Instead they flip an ignition switch and push a starter button.

Stripped of trim, lights, and glass, the cars are plastered with sponsors' decals. The numbered cars are painted different colors. Jeff Gordon's number 24 Chevrolet features bright red, yellow, and blue paint. Unlike family cars, race cars don't

Jeff Gordon inspects Jimmie Johnson's Chevrolet while mechanics work on the car at the Lowe's Motor Speedway in Concord, North Carolina. At one time NASCAR race cars were very similar to the vehicles ordinary people could buy from auto dealers. This is why they were called "stock cars." However, vehicles used in NASCAR events today are built only for racing.

have **speedometers** to show drivers how fast they are going. It doesn't matter. They only need to be faster than the other drivers!

(Go back to page 14.)

Drive-through Service

Behind every great driver is a great pit crew. The crew's speed and ability help a driver win races. The crew's mistakes cost the driver precious time.

Because race cars travel so fast, they guzzle gas and batter tires. When a driver stops to fuel up and change tires, it's the pit crew's job to get the car back on the track as fast as possible. Jeff Gordon's crew takes fewer than 15 seconds. One crewmember jacks up the 3,400-pound car in just one stroke. Two others heave the four 70-pound tires, and two others quickly install them. Other team members clean debris off the car and fill up the 22-gallon tank with gas from cans that weigh 80 pounds apiece when they are full.

A driver usually makes eight pit stops during a race, so the crew must be both fast and strong. They train by working out in gyms. They also practice working together to become a fast, efficient team.

Communicating with each other and the driver is important. A crew chief oversees the team. During the race, the driver and the crew chief talk on headsets about how the car is running and discuss strategies. A first-rate team and an ace driver is a tough combination to beat. (Go back to page 15.) ◀◀

Members of a pit crew must do a lot in a very short amount of time. According to NASCAR rules, only seven people are allowed to work on the race car during a pit stop. It typically takes the pit crew 12 to 16 seconds to replace four worn tires and fill the car with fuel.

In the Driver's Seat

During a NASCAR race, 43 cars speed at well over 100 mph around the same track. Small mistakes can cost a driver more than just the race, however. They can potentially cause multi-car wrecks and dangerous track conditions. Amazingly, though, because of many safety precautions, drivers often walk away from serious accidents.

Inside the car, a metal cage and padded roll bars protect the driver. Instead of glass, the windshield is made from clear, shatterproof plastic, and the driver's side window is covered with heavy padded webbing. Cars also feature rooftop escape hatches. The car's seat wraps around the driver's rib cage and shoulders.

Each driver wears a seatbelt harness and a **HANS device**, or collar that protects the head and neck.

From the tops of their heads to the tips of their toes, special clothing also keeps drivers safe. They wear flame-retardant suits, gloves, socks, and shoes to prevent possible burns. Strong, lightweight, helmets protect their heads.

To keep drivers safe during a race, officials signal them with warning flags that indicate accidents or dangers, like oil spills. While car racing may seem risky, today's drivers speed around the track wearing much safer gear and driving much safer cars than ever before.

(Go back to page 18.) ◀◀

A window net hangs over the side of Jeff's car. Before the race, the net will be snapped into position. NASCAR rules require safety nets on the windows. They keep the driver's arms from flying out the window if the car crashes or rolls. Safety features on race cars help keep NASCAR drivers as safe as possible.

Legendary Racers

Throughout the history of NASCAR, many drivers have stood in Victory Lane. Some families have produced generations of drivers, passing the tradition down from father to son to grandson. Among many aces, Richard Petty, Bobby Allison, and Dale Earnhardt Sr. stand out as racing greats.

Richard Petty's career began in 1958. Nicknamed "The King," he set many records: wins (200), top-five finishes (555), top-ten finishes (712), consecutive races won (10), and more. He captured the championship seven times and drove 300,000 miles in competitions. His 35-year career is the longest ever. Other Pettys who raced include Richard's father, Lee; his son, Kyle; and Kyle's son, Adam, who was killed in a race in 2000.

Bobby Allison's career started in 1965. In 23 years, he won 85 races and had 336 top-five and 446 top-ten finishes. A three-time Daytona 500 winner, Allison won the championship once. Other Allison family drivers include Clifford, Davey, and Donnie.

Dale Earnhardt Sr.'s career began in 1975. Fans called him "The Intimidator" or "The Man in Black" because of his aggressive driving and tough attitude. Earnhardt captured 76 wins and seven championships. A NASCAR hero, Earnhardt's death at the 2001 Daytona 500 stunned the racing world. Fans will never forget the legendary driver of car number 3. Other Earnhardt racers include Ralph and Dale Jr.

(Go back to page 23.)

Training to Race

For most people a 500-mile car trip takes about eight hours. It takes NASCAR drivers less than half that time. Many people don't realize that drivers do more than sit and steer. Racing is tough on their bodies and their minds.

During races, drivers use as much energy as long-distance runners. At the turns, their cars endure forces like a space shuttle during liftoff. Temperatures inside the cockpit reach more than 130°F. By the end of a typical race, Jeff has lost 8 pounds, and his eyes ache. Despite the physical strain, drivers need to concentrate and make split-second decisions.

At 5'8" and 150 pounds, Jeff is lighter than other drivers, giving him an edge. He still trains, however. In addition to running practice laps, many drivers lift weights, run, and eat well.

NASCAR drivers need good hand-eye coordination, which is the ability to react quickly to what they see. To improve their reaction time, some drivers play video games. In racing games, they can "drive" on specific tracks, which helps them become familiar with the track. Fans sometimes race their favorite drivers through online games, and some have even moved on to racing real cars. Imagine beating Jeff on a virtual race track!

(Go back to page 31.) ◀◀

Sports Speak

Every sport has its own vocabulary. Car racing is no different. Special words and phrases describe everything from the car to the crew to racing tactics.

The final hour of practice before the race is *happy hour*. Everyone hopes their car will be *hooked-up*, or performing well, instead of being *junk*, or doing poorly. During the race, the driver will be *on the throttle*, going as fast as possible. He'll look for the best route around the track, *the groove*, and *get under* opponents, passing them on the inside at the turns. He'll hope to avoid a *parking lot*, a multi-car crash, so he doesn't get a *DNF*, or *did not finish*.

When the driver stops, the pit crew will put on *fresh rubber*, meaning new tires. A *wrench*, or car mechanic, might use some *200 mph tape*, strong enough to hold a damaged car together. One crew member cleans off any *marbles*, or debris. Sometimes the stop can be a *gas-and-go*, meaning just fueling up.

At the end of the race, there might be a *shoot out*, with two or more drivers racing to the end. Each one hopes to get to *Victory Lane*, which is the winner's circle.

(Go back to page 33.)

A Spectator Sport

At first it was just a few friends sitting in bleachers watching a race. Now, over six million people attend NASCAR races each year, while over 275 million more around the world watch on television. One race can have more spectators in attendance than a World Series game, a professional basketball game, and the Super Bowl combined.

Fans travel across the country to attend races, paying from $100 to $1,000 per ticket. Some tracks hold 250,000 people. At Talladega Superspeedway in Alabama, workers bring in truckloads of food and beverages to feed the crowds. By the end of the day, spectators have consumed over 9,000 gallons of soft drinks and more than 12,000 pounds of hot dogs. Spread tip-to-tip, that many hot dogs would easily circle the 2.66-mile track. Fans also spend over one billion dollars every year buying NASCAR hats, shirts, decals, and more.

With the chance to reach such large audiences, companies pay drivers to advertise on their race cars. DuPont sponsors Jeff Gordon's car, and his many other sponsors range from Quaker State motor oil to Pepsi. Whatever the sponsor, NASCAR fans are devoted to their favorite drivers and love to cheer them on as they speed around the track.

(Go back to page 41.)

Women in NASCAR

Many professional sports, such as football and baseball, began with men as the primary competitors. That includes car racing. While most race car drivers today are men, over the years women have also climbed behind the wheel. Most of them have been Indy racers, driving cars with open wheels, instead of stock cars. Today's most famous female driver is Indy racer Danica Patrick. In April of 2008, she became the first woman to win an Indy Car series race.

Only 14 women have ever driven in NASCAR's Sprint Cup series. The most successful, Janet Guthrie, competed in 33 races in the late 1970s. Most recently Shawna Robinson competed in a Sprint Cup race in 2002. Others, like Chrissy Wallace, currently are excelling in other NASCAR series.

In 1993 Lyn St. James, a two-time Indy 500 driver, established a program to train female drivers. So far, 150 women from 38 states and two countries have taken part. NASCAR also started a diversity program to encourage female and minority drivers.

Three top female race car drivers today are (left to right) Melanie Troxel, Danica Patrick, and Leilani Munter. Melanie competes in NHRA drag-racing events, while Danica and Leilani race Indy cars. Only 14 women have competed at the highest level of NASCAR competition. The most recent was Shawna Robinson, who participated in several Winston Cup races during 2001 and 2002.

In April of 2008, following Danica Patrick's historic win, members from one NASCAR racing team approached her about racing stock cars. Who knows, maybe someday soon a woman will challenge Jeff Gordon for the checkered flag.

(Go back to page 41.)

1971   Jeffrey Michael Gordon is born on August 4 in Vallejo, California.

1976   At age 5, Jeff begins racing Quarter Midget cars.

1979   Jeff wins the national championship in Quarter Midget racing.

1981   After switching to go-kart racing, Jeff wins four championships.

1986   The Gordons move to Pittsboro, Indiana, and Jeff begins racing sprint cars.

1990   Jeff becomes the youngest winner of the USAC Midget Championship; attends the Buck Baker Driving School; starts racing stock cars.

1994   In May, Jeff captures his first Winston Cup series win at the Coca-Cola 600; wins the first Brickyard 400; marries Brooke Sealey.

1995   Jeff wins the Southern 500 and his first Winston Cup championship title.

1997   In February, he becomes the youngest driver to win the Daytona 500; wins the Southern 500; clinches his second Winston Cup title.

1998   Jeff wins the Coca-Cola 600, the Southern 500, and the Brickyard 400; claims his third Winston Cup title.

2001   Dale Earnhardt Sr. is killed in an accident at the Daytona 500; Jeff wins the Brickyard 400; captures his fourth Winston Cup title, becoming only the third person in history and the youngest to claim more than three titles.

2005   Jeff wins the Daytona 500; people talk of a "slump" after Jeff finishes in 11th place; begins working with crew chief Steve Letarte.

2006   In November Jeff marries Ingrid Vandebosch; becomes a co-founder of Athletes for Hope foundation; funds the Jeff Gordon Children's Hospital.

2007   Daughter Ella Sofia is born in May; Jeff claims six wins, 21 top-five, and 30 top-ten finishes; ends the season ranking second; becomes sixth on all-time wins list; holds the longest streak of winning at least one race for 14 consecutive seasons.

2008   Dale Earnhardt Jr. joins Jeff on the Hendrick Motorsports team.

Selected Awards

1993 NASCAR Rookie of the Year

1996 The Leukemia and Lymphoma Society Special Recognition Award

1998 *USA Weekend Magazine* Most Caring Athlete

1999 The Leukemia and Lymphoma Society Dr. William Dameshek Award

2001 True Value Man of the Year

2002 *GQ* Athlete of the Year

2003 *Sporting News* NASCAR Good Guys Award

2005 *Sporting News* NASCAR Good Guys Award

2006 *Sporting News* NASCAR Good Guys Giver Award
Make-A-Wish Society of Joy Award
Make-A-Wish Society of Strength Award
Champions for Life Award (The Marrow Foundation/Hendricks Marrow Program)

2007 The deVilliers Society Award (The Leukemia and Lymphoma Society)

Selected Accomplishments

1994 Brickyard 400 winner

1995 Winston Cup Champion
Southern 500 winner
Champion of the Nextel All-Star Challenge

1996 Southern 500 winner

1997 Winston Cup Champion
Daytona 500 winner
Southern 500 winner
Champion of the Nextel All-Star Challenge

1998 Winston Cup Champion
Brickyard 400 winner
Southern 500 winner

1999 Daytona 500 winner

2001 Winston Cup Champion
Brickyard 400 winner
Champion of the Nextel All-Star Challenge

2002 Southern 500 winner

2004 Brickyard 400 winner

2005 Daytona 500 winner

Four-time Winston No Bull 5 Winner

Nine victories on road courses

Career Statistics

Year	Wins	Finished in Top 5	Rank	Earnings
1993	0	7	14th	$765, 168
1994	2	7	8th	$1,779,523
1995	7	17	1st	$4,347,343
1996	10	21	2nd	$3,428,485
1997	10	22	1st	$6,375,658
1998	13	26	1st	$9,306,584
1999	7	18	6th	$5,858,633
2000	3	11	9th	$3,001,144
2001	6	18	1st	$10,879,757
2002	3	13	4th	$6,154,475
2003	3	12	4th	$5,107,760
2004	5	11	3rd	$6,437,660
2005	4	4	11th	$6,855,440
2006	2	11	6th	$5,975,870
2007	6	15	2nd	$7,148,620
2008*	0	7	6th	$2,720,991
Total	83	216		$84,579,850

*Through June of 2008

Books and Periodicals

Gordon, Jeff. *Racing Back to the Front—My Memoir*. New York: Atria Books, 2003.

Grissom, Glen. *Jeff Gordon: The NASCAR Superstar's Story*. St. Paul: Motorbooks International, 2005

Leebrick, Krystal. *Jeff Gordon*. Mankato, MN: Capstone Press, 2004.

Miller, Timothy and Steve Milton. *NASCAR Now!* New York: Firefly Books, 2006.

Ryan, Nate. "For Gordon, It's All About Winning." *USA Today* (November 11, 2006): Sports section.

Savage, Jeff. *Jeff Gordon*. Minneapolis: First Avenue Editions, 2007.

Schaefer, A. R. *The History of NASCAR*. Mankato, MN: Capstone Press, 2005.

Web Sites

http://www.nascar.com

The National Association for Stock Car Auto Racing (NASCAR) has acted as the governing body of car racing since 1948. Its Web site includes news items, descriptions of races, driver profiles, tips about racing, and current rankings.

http://www.jeffgordon.com

The official Web site for Jeff Gordon provides a short biography, his career statistics and accomplishments, recent news, and information about his crew.

http://www.jeffgordonfoundation.com

Information about the mission and programs of the Jeff Gordon Foundation, including news about upcoming events, can be viewed at this official Web site.

http://www.hendrickmotorsports.com

The organization Hendrick Motorsports owns four racing teams, including Jeff Gordon's. The official Web site offers information about the company, its history, successes, teams, race cars, and pit crews.

http://www.nascarhalloffame.com

The Web site for the new NASCAR Hall of Fame includes information about the building's opening in 2010, along with news about inductees, events, and a description of the museum.

checkered flag—a black and white flag waved when the winner crosses the finish line.

HANS device—a U-shaped collar that straps to a driver's helmet and protects the head and neck from injury.

horsepower—an engine's or motor's power, measured by its ability to move 33,000 pounds the distance of one foot in one minute.

infield—the inner portion of a race track.

lap—one circle around a racetrack.

leukemia—a form of cancer that affects the blood and bone marrow.

pit crew—the team that fuels a race car, changes its tires, and makes repairs during a race.

pole position—the best starting position on a race track, on the inside of the front row, won by the driver with the fastest time in a qualifying race.

qualifying race—a prerace competition to determine which drivers will compete in the main race.

rookie—a beginner or first-year player in a sport.

speedometer—a device on a car that displays how many miles per hour (mph) a car is traveling.

sponsor—a company that pays an athlete to publicly support its product.

Sprint Cup series—the 36 NASCAR races in which drivers compete to earn points toward winning the championship, called the Sprint Cup, formerly known as the Nextel Cup and the Winston Cup.

standings—the list of drivers arranged from first to last by the number of points each one wins during the season.

stock car—a standard car that can be modified for racing.

streak—a period of either good or bad luck, such as a winning or losing streak.

superspeedway—a racetrack that is longer than two miles.

Victory Lane—a section in the infield where the winning driver celebrates his or her victory.

page 8 "We've been put . . . " Jeff Gordon, *Racing Back to the Front—My Memoir* (New York: Atria Books, 2003), 153.

page 8 "This championship . . . " Glen Grissom, *Jeff Gordon: The NASCAR Superstar's Story* (St. Paul: Motorbooks International, 2005), 143.

page 12 "When I was . . . " Gordon, *Racing Back to the Front—My Memoir*, 20.

page 14 "I loved stock car . . . " Ibid., 42.

page 14 "I'd like to . . . " Ibid., 79.

page 16 "I've had to learn . . ." Mark Zeske, "The Need for Speed," *Boys' Life* 86, no. 5 (May 1996), 22.

page 18 "I'll tell you . . . " Jeff Gordon, *Jeff Gordon: Burning Up the Track* (Champaign, IL: Sports Publishing LLC, 2003), 51.

page 20 "We slept . . . " Jerry Adler, "Chariots of Fire," *Newsweek* 130, no. 4 (July 28, 1997), 54.

page 20 "I am . . . " George Tiedemann, *Trading Paint: Dale Earnhardt vs. Jeff Gordon* (New York: Bishop Books, 2001), 9–10.

page 23 "We all would . . . " Tiedemann, Ibid., 70.

page 25 "Jeff Gordon makes . . . " Lee Spencer, "Meet the Four-Time Champ—He's 30 Now," *Sporting News* 225, no. 48 (November 26, 2001), 20.

page 26 "You go through times . . ." "Gordon Savors Bristol Win," *The St. Petersburg* (Florida) *Times* (August 26, 2002), 2C.

page 28 "If you get up . . . " Lars Anderson, "Here Comes Mr. Gordon," *Sports Illustrated* 107, no. 1 (July 2, 2007), 65

page 29 "There's no doubt . . ." Mark Bechtel, "Inside Motor Sports," *Sports Illustrated* 97, no. 3 (July 15, 2002), 139.

page 30 "If my experience . . . " Gordon, *Racing Back to the Front—My Memoir*, 221.

page 32 "I'm looking..." Mark Bechtel, "Here He Comes," *Sports Illustrated* 97, no. 3 (July 15, 2002), 139.

page 35 "One thing I'd . . . " Gordon, *Racing Back to the Front—My Memoir*, 217–218.

page 38 "Steve could dissect . . . " Anderson, "Here Comes Mr. Gordon," 66.

page 39 "It's humbling to . . . " NASCAR Official Release, "Gordon 200 and Counting for Make-A-Wish Efforts," NASCAR Official Web site (April 11, 2008). http://www.nascar.com/2008/news/headlines/official/04/11/jgordon.make.a.wish/index.html

page 41 "I'm in the . . . " Anderson, "Here Comes Mr. Gordon," 70.

page 46 "Being a parent . . ." "Sonoma Holds Special Meaning for Gordon." Hendrick Motorsports Official Web site (June 17, 2008). http://www.hendrickmotorsports.com/news_detail.asp?id=2049

page 47 "From Nobody . . . " Gordon, *Racing Back to the Front—My Memoir*, 84–85.

Numbers in **bold italics** refer to captions.

Kerrily Sapet is the author of numerous biographies and articles for young adults. While writing this book, she and her family toured the famed Brickyard.

PICTURE CREDITS

page

1: Tag Heuer/NMI

4: Atlanta Journal/KRT

7: TV Guide/NMI

9: IOS Photos

10: John Mahoney/Ramona Oil Co./PRMS

13: Blaues Schiff/IOW Photos

15: Madame Tussauds/NMI

16: Detroit Press Press/KRT

19: Shelly Katz/Getty Images

21: Erik Campos/The State/KRT

22: FPS/NMI

24: TV Guide/NMI

26: Orlando Sentinel/KRT

29: Sparkle/PRMS

30: Macon Telegraph/KRT

33: Stock Car Racing/NMI

34: Pepsi/NMI

36: Texas Motor Speedway/PRMS

39: Bristol/PRMS

40: Orlando Sentinel/KRT

42: The State/MCT

44: New Millennium Images

45: Fort Worth Star-Telegram/KRT

46: Detroit Free Press/MCT

48: IOS Photos

49: BMS/FPS

50: Nazareth Racecam/PRMS

51: Getty Images for NASCAR

52: Sparkle/PRMS

55: Interstate Bakeries Corp./NMI

Front cover: Sparkle/PRMS